# KK Loves Gymnastics

Story by Kylie Renee Reid

Illustrations by Laura Acosta

TDR Brands Publishing

Printed in the United States of America

ISBN 978-0-9988804-2-6

Thank you Coach Brittney for being a great coach.

KK Loves Gymnastics

# KK Loves Gymnastics

Once upon a time, there was a girl named KK. She loved gymnastics. Although she loved to swim, run, and cheer, gymnastics was her favorite!

She loved it so much. She asked if she could join the official team to compete. Her mom had a long talk with her to make sure she was up for the challenge. She said, "YES!"

KK made up her mind that she would do her best. She began to practice five hours a week on Tuesdays and Thursdays. Coach Brittany had a long talk with KK about all the things she would need to learn, but most of all she wanted her to have FUN!

Coach Brittney explained that this sport would challenge her and that practices would prepare her to perform in front of a large crowd in the fall.

"Once you learn the basic bends, jumps, and flips, you will even begin to do awesome floor routines."

*WOW!* KK thought to herself. *This is going to be amazing. I am going to try my very best.*

She learned the importance of stretching before you begin to help with your flexibility.

KK watched older kid gymnasts walk the beams and flip with such grace. She was so inspired by them. One day she would be able to do that too.

She knew she would need to focus, get plenty of rest, and work extra hard.

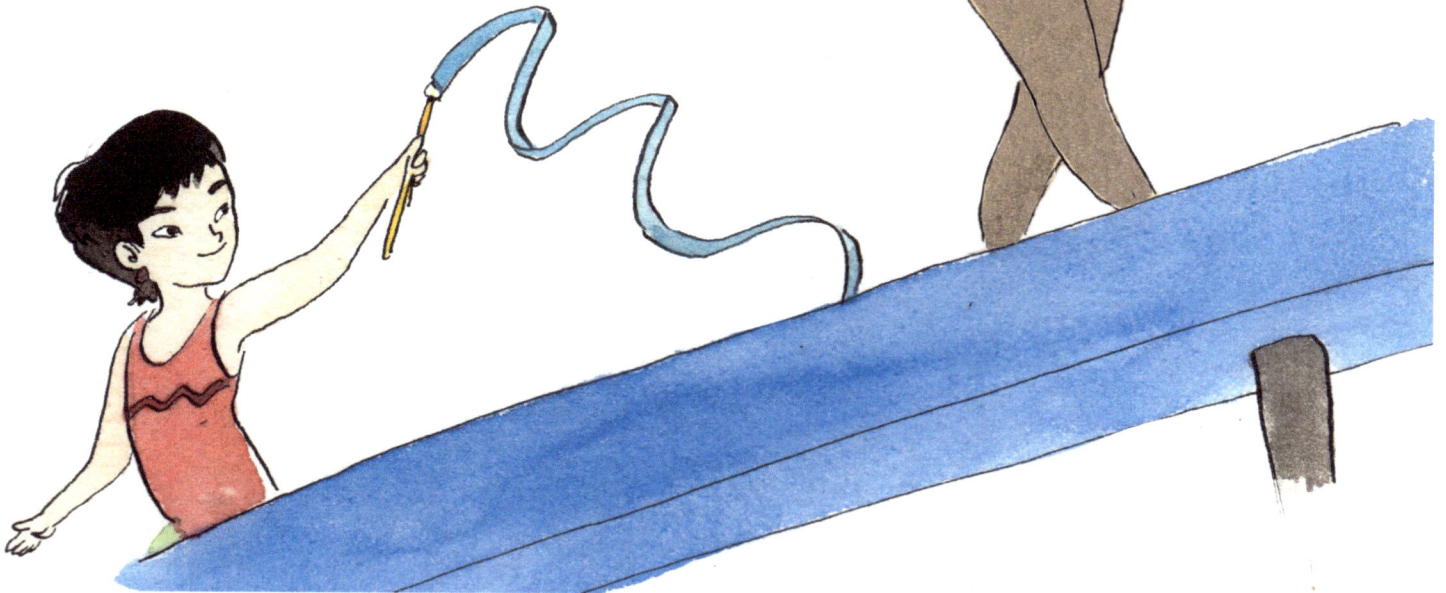

During practice, KK and her friends encouraged each other and talked about their fears. Even if you fall or make a mistake, it is okay. They learned to share their feelings openly and never give up. After practicing for a couple of hours, they always took a break and ate a healthy snack.

Eating healthy gave them more energy to perform their very best. KK's favorite snack was fruit cups!

After each meal, the girls always washed their hands and ran back into the gym for round two. If they worked really hard, Coach Brittney even let them have free time to jump in the trampoline pit!

KK and her friends loved to bounce in the hole! It was the best reward after practicing and giving their best.

After practice had ended, KK headed home with her family and smiled as she looked out of the window. She imagined herself performing in the fall. She was so grateful to have new friends and a kid coach. Although she would have to work very hard, she was up for the challenge.

If you are thinking about gymnastics, KK says give it a try! She absolutely loves it, and she hopes you will too.

The End

## About the author

My name is Kylie and I love to cook. I was born in Atlanta Georgia, but I want to see the world. Once I started writing this book, I decided to write more. I hope that you enjoy them and I hope they make you smile. I was a little nervous at first, but I'm starting to get the hang of it. When I'm not writing or cooking, I'm usually spending time with my family, at gymnastics practice, or watching cool DIY videos on YouTube!

www.ingramcontent.com/pod-product-compliance
Lightning Source LLC
Chambersburg PA
CBHW042120040426

42449CB00002B/116